THEY DIED TOO YOUNG

KAREN CARPENTER

Tom Stockdale

CHELSEA HOUSE PUBLISHERS
Philadelphia

First published in traditional hardback edition
©2000 by Chelsea House Publishers.

Printed in Malaysia.
First Printing
1 3 5 7 9 8 6 4 2

Copyright © Parragon Book Service Ltd 1995
Unit 13–17, Avonbridge Trading Estate, Atlantic Road
Avonmouth, Bristol, England BS11 9QD

Illustrations courtesy of: Aquarius; Hulton Deutsch Collection;
Mirror Syndication International

Library of Congress Cataloging-in-Publication Data
Stockdale, Tom.
       Karen Carpenter / Tom Stockdale.
           cm.—(They died too young)
       Includes index.
       Summary: Describes the childhood and music career of the lead
    singer of the Carpenters, a popular singing duo in the 1970s, and
    her early death from heart failure, the result of years of suffering
    with anorexia nervosa.
       ISBN 0-7910-5225-7 (hc)
       1. Carpenter, Karen, 1950-1983 Juvenile literature.   2. Singers—
    United States—Biography—Juvenile literature.   [1. Carpenter,
    Karen, 1950-1983   2. Singers.   3. Carpenters (Musical group).
    4. Anorexia nervosa.   5. Women—Biography.]   I. Title.
    II. Series.
    ML3930.C263S76   1999
    782.42164'092—dc21
    [B]   99-21160
                                                                        CIP

CONTENTS

Richard and Karen Carpenter

WE'VE ONLY JUST BEGUN

Agnes Carpenter was almost eight months pregnant when she and her husband, Harold, moved into their newly built house in New Haven, Connecticut, in August 1946. Their first child, Richard Lynne, was already showing signs of an unusually sensitive musical ear three and a half years later, when his parents presented him with a sister. Karen Anne Carpenter was born on March 2, 1950, a time of hope and hard work for the average American.

Money was not plentiful, and despite Harold's career, the Carpenters had to count every penny. Agnes kept a meticulously tidy house, and the couple ran a car-washing business to make a little extra cash.

Both Harold and Agnes were music lovers, and young Richard's musical inclinations were fostered as much as they could afford. His taste was molded partly by the few records his parents had, an eclectic mixture of military and orchestral music. Karen, meanwhile, was a more active child who took dance lessons and was a nimble acrobat: she was literally tickled off a trapeze when she was four, causing a bad wound to her lip. The children spent a lot of time together, and it was Karen who would defend Richard at school when he was picked on for his shyness.

She was the extrovert, enjoying games in the street and becoming a good basketball player, while Richard stayed in listening to music. It was Karen who did a paper route, not her older brother. Her admiration of him, however, often led her to join him in his listening, so she was naturally drawn to his musical interests. The family kept a variety of pets, which suited Karen's kind nature; she developed a love of Disney characters which would become a lifelong obsession.

The two children were influenced most strongly by their mother, who was a tower of strength in the neighborhood. Agnes was a devoutly moral and hardworking woman and never forgot a friend in need. She and Harold were dedicated to Richard and Karen, but it was Richard's musical potential which took precedence, mainly because it was so all-consuming. By the age of nine he had developed an instinctive musical ear, whether listening to records or to the new rock 'n' roll sounds that had exploded onto the radio. The arrival of Bill Haley on the music scene brought a whole new flavor to the airwaves, and Richard seemed able to lap up both the old and new.

During their "listening sessions" he and Karen studied and sang along to everything, building a solid musical foundation. Richard's piano lessons were the beginning of his musical training, and by the time he was 12, it was apparent that his talent lay beyond the straightforward sight-reading scales. A year later, he passed an audition for the School of Music at Yale University, and at 15 he was in demand with local groups. Shortly after, he cut his first record as pianist for a local band, the Barries.

Karen's pattern of musical development was less precocious. She toyed with the accordion and the flute but was usually distracted by some outdoor pursuit.

As she moved into her teen years, she lost the baby fat which had been the cause of some teasing at school. Her developing figure included the wide hips which would

Brother and sister

become the main focus of her future self-loathing. She had several strong friendships as well as her relationship with Richard, who was very much a loner by inclination, and she seemed as normal as any other teenage girl.

In June 1963 the family moved to Downey, California, a peaceful suburb of Los Angeles. Harold Carpenter had been eager to move for some time because of the guaranteed sunshine, but he and Agnes were also well aware of the advantages it offered the 16-year-old Richard. The first year there was a financial struggle. It took that long to sell their New Haven house, and during that time they were paying rent as well as the mortgage.

There were few advantages for Karen in the upheaval. She was saddened by the loss of her Connecticut friends, and to some extent she took refuge in food. It must have been difficult for her to watch the swift progress of her brother, who was playing the organ in the local church as well as performing in a jazz band. The emergence of the Beatles and the Beach Boys influenced him to move toward writing popular music, for here was something seriously popular which he could understand intellectually as well as musically.

It is often said that everyone has a musical instrument to which they are naturally inclined: the trick is to find it. Karen was lucky when she discovered the drums. She persuaded her doubting parents to buy her a drum set and, in 1964, repaid their faith by practicing for hours with the drummer from the school marching band. Her diligence paid off, and discovering a natural sense of rhythm, she quickly picked up the various techniques.

Despite this, Karen's first public appearance was as a singer, in a competition which Richard had entered with an original song. There they met Wes Jacobs, another entrant, who Richard invited to participate in some informal sessions at the Carpenter house. They worked hard, and found themselves a niche playing at local dances as the Richard

8   *They Died Too Young*

Carpenter Trio. Karen came across as an oddity: a girl who sang and played the drums at the same time. Although she had good pitch and tone, there seemed nothing remarkable about her voice at this time. She thought of herself as a drummer first and foremost, and it would take Richard's more mature, later musical arrangements for the lasting qualities of her voice to appear.

Meanwhile, Richard was advancing his musical studies at California State University, Long Beach, and greatly impressed Frank Pooler, the head of choral studies, with his playing. Richard took his 16-year-old sister to Pooler for some singing advice, and he was struck with her natural vocal style. She gained a soloist's place in the university choir, and she and Richard gathered a growing reputation around the campus, as well as in the town, where the Carpenter Trio was playing as often as possible.

Richard Carpenter at the piano

TICKET TO RIDE

Richard was used to accompanying singer friends on the piano when they auditioned, so it was not a surprise when Dan Friberg requested his services in May 1966. The audition was held at the garage studio of well-known bassist Joe Osborne, who co-owned a small recording label, and Richard took Karen along to observe. During the course of the evening Karen was asked to sing a number, and the reaction to her recording was one of amazement. Karen's voice seemed to have an attraction all of its own to the magnetic tape. She was soon signed to Osborne's label, Magic Lamp, and a single was released of two of Richard's compositions, "Looking for Love" and "I'll Be Yours." Though it did not meet with any commercial success, it was a first step on the ladder which would take the Carpenters to the very top.

Progress for the Carpenter Trio was swift. They appeared in a "Battle of the Bands" held at the Hollywood Bowl in June 1966 and were described in the *Los Angeles Times* review as "the musical surprise of the evening." Their success brought a record deal and a test with RCA Records, but the traditional style of the tracks did not strike the right note with the company, and they were released from their contract.

In the meantime, Richard had met John Bettis, a hippy non-conformist whose outlook was a world away from Richard's traditional attitude, but whose surprisingly romantic lyrical style impressed him. They started to work together, two different creative talents finding a common goal in music. Richard then recruited a guitarist, bass player, and vocalist, and they rehearsed together under several names until the name Spectrum stuck. Their demo tapes were uninfluenced by contemporary pop charts, and even though record companies were looking for acts to rival the impact of the Motown dance sound, Richard's unwavering confidence carried in singer Ed Sulzer, who offered to take their tapes around to record companies, and also helped Spectrum to find gigs. With their blue velvet suits and close harmony songs, they were a polished, if dated, group, in danger of not fitting into any recognizable musical category with their "choral approach to pop," as Richard called it.

Karen's musical confidence seemed to grow without her having to work at it, and she continued with other interests outside the regular rehearsals and gigs. So while Richard was always playing or teaching one of the pupils he took on to help with some expenses, Karen had some time for a normal teenage life. She had her first boyfriend when she was 16, and within a year was worried enough about her personal appearance to go on a strict water diet. She lost more than 14 pounds and in 1968 started dating Spectrum's guitarist, Gary Sims. But she still seemed overly concerned about the parts of her body that she could not change.

The same year also brought the end of Spectrum, even though they had come very close to being signed by a couple of small labels. With the contractual discussions had come talk of money, and Richard's insistence on receiving a higher percentage (which seemed only natural to him as the band's driving musical force), had resulted in the band splitting up. Richard and Karen returned to Joe Osborne's studio and recorded several tracks, layering the vocals themselves. The uncomplicated sound suited them and proved itself at an audition for the television talent program *Your All-American College Show,* for which they simply called themselves the

The Carpenters

Carpenters. Their confidence was boosted by three appearances in all on the program (which included Henry Mancini on the judging panel), as well as the publicity gained from national exposure.

Their commercial potential was recognized by John and Tom Bahler, who had been hired by Ford Motors to find musicians to help promote a new car, and they signed a $50,000 deal early in 1969. The contract helped to offset their disappointment at their continued lack of success in finding a record company. Two things were to change their luck. Firstly, the underlying trend in pop music moved away from the production team method of songwriting, used so successfully by Phil Spector and Motown, to the singer/songwriter style begun by the Beatles and about to hit America in the form of Simon & Garfunkel, with an emphasis on the album format rather than the single. Secondly, through Jack Daugherty, trumpeter and friend of Ed Sulzer, the Carpenters demo found its way to Herb Alpert, leader of the Tijuana Brass and the "A" of A&M Records.

Although A&M was primarily known for its rock artists, including Procul Harem and Free, it also had a core of more traditional songwriting talent headed by Burt Bacharach. Alpert recognized the qualities of the arrangements on the demo tape and was struck by the warmth of Karen's vocals. And just as he wasn't afraid of signing bands at the cutting edge of pop music if he could hear quality, he was willing to gamble on a sound that, to most of his music business contemporaries, had all the hallmarks of nostalgia. On April 22, 1969, 22-year-old Richard and 19-year-old Karen signed a contract with A&M. They managed to talk their way out of the deal with Ford and began work on an album.

Their hours of rehearsing at home had prepared them for the long sessions in the studio, breaking only for fast-food snacks late at night. By October 1969, the album, entitled *Offering,* and produced by Jack Daugherty, was ready to release. The first single, a cover of the Beatles' "Ticket to

Karen performing on the drums

Ride," reached a respectable number 54 on the charts, but the album went nowhere. The bland image of the Carpenters counted against them with the critics, especially in view of the label they were signed to, but Alpert had not taken them on for quick commercial success. He gave them his backing to continue, despite the teasing he got from his music business contemporaries.

The Carpenters then received a golden opportunity from Burt Bacharach who, without knowing they were label stable-mates, inquired about their version of "Ticket to Ride." The upshot was a meeting for Richard and Karen with Burt—one of their heroes—and the offer of performing a Bachrach med-ley as the opening spot at a benefit gig he was playing in February 1970. While Richard was working on the songs for the medley, Alpert pushed an old Bachrach/David song, "They Love to Be Close to You," at him and convinced him to do something with it. The resulting session sent a buzz around the company, and it was decided to chance Richard's slow, lush arrangement as one half of a double "A"-sided single, with the long original title shortened by parentheses to "(They Long to Be) Close to You." Radio play was instant and concentrated on the Bachrach cover, and the record-buying public went wild over the very qualities the critics were ridiculing. In August, the single went to number one in America, keeping both Bread ("Make It with You") and Stevie Wonder ("Signed Sealed Delivered I'm Yours") off the top. It went to number six in Britain, where Freda Payne's "Band of Gold" was number one.

The chart success put more pressure on the hardworking pair. Their management was still organized partly by Karen, even when it was taken over by Sherwin Bash, a seasoned professional. Karen was used to running the day-to-day affairs of the band while Richard worked on the musical input, and she had her mother's ability to be direct in her dealing with people. She was talkative by nature and made an agreeable counter to the more introspective Richard.

As the band began a heavy touring schedule that would

They Died Too Young

continue into the future, Karen continued her habit of having personal relationships with the Carpenters' entourage, going steady with their road manager, Jerry Luby. Her personal life would always be influenced by the image she seemed to have of the right sort of man for her, combined with a need to find a man who, as she became increasingly wealthy, also had financial independence.

The idea for the follow-up to "Close to You" came to Richard by a curious route. The A&M writing partnership of Roger Nichols and Paul Williams had written a song for a bank commercial, which Richard heard on television and knew would work with Karen's voice. "We've Only Just Begun" was their second hit in a row, confirming public recognition of Karen's voice as the perfect vehicle for the bittersweet sentiments of the Carpenters' music.

The follow-up album to *Offering* was recorded and packaged as quickly as possible so as to capitalize on the success of the single, and Richard, who was already producing in all but name, had grasped how to fit Karen's velvet vocals around the framework of his arrangements. The inevitably titled *Close to You* was a strong seller, with tracks including "Maybe It's You" and the country classic "Reason to Believe." It would go on to sell five million copies, and it consolidated the Carpenters' position at A&M. At the 1970 Grammy Awards, Richard and Karen reaped two awards from six nominations: Best New Artist and Best Contemporary Vocal Group.

With success came wealth, though Richard and Karen took the financial rewards pretty much in stride. Their focus was on the songs, and it was with some reluctance that they took A&M's advice to employ professional accountants, rather than continuing to let Agnes look after the books. In any case, they were too busy to rest on their laurels. At their public appearances they both found it difficult to come to terms with the fact that Karen, as the singer, was seen as the star. During interviews she would regularly stress Richard's place as the creator of the music which was bringing her so

Richard and Karen

much fan mail, although he was quite happy at the beginning just to see his music selling so well.

He was aware of the importance of visual presentation at their concerts and managed to convince Karen to come out from behind her drums, at least for the ballads. It was difficult for her to come to terms with leading the band, as she was not a natural "showman," but whether she liked it or not, she *was* the voice of the Carpenters.

The band made 1971 their own with a continuation of singles success. "For All We Know," released in March, and which Richard and Karen first heard on the soundtrack of the film *Lovers and Other Strangers*, was followed three months later with "Rainy Days and Mondays," which became their fourth top-five hit. This string of successes was completed by "Superstar," which had already sold a million copies for Rita Coolidge. Karen's soulful reading got it a second gold record, and it was kept from the number one spot only by Rod Stewart's "Maggie May."

These singles made up the album of hits which they called simply *Carpenters*. It had great depth of quality, stemming from Richard's exacting craftsmanship and Karen's perfect pitch. The album also included "Sometimes," a track written for them by the judge from *Your All-American College Show*, Henry Mancini, which was about as high a compliment as Richard and Karen could imagine. Mancini was full of praise for both of them, making it clear that he was giving them the song because he knew they could create the definitive version.

Nineteen seventy one also included an eight-week television show called *Make Your Own Kind of Music*, a showcase for new talent in which Karen and Richard appeared as the highlight of each episode. Their standing within the music industry was made official at the Grammy Awards: from its four nominations, *Carpenters* walked away with the Best Album Award.

Karen framed by her drum set

TOP OF THE WORLD

The enthusiasm of the Carpenters' fans was not shared by critics, who seemed to take exception to stars who insisted on being average people. It was hard to abuse their music, which, considering their popularity, would come across as sour grapes and would be criticizing a line of popular songwriting that went back to Irving Berlin and Cole Porter. The criticism was centered upon Richard and Karen's personal style, their clean living, and the fact that they were proud conformists. They were simply incapable of the rebellion which was expected of young artists in the music business, and the fact that they got fan mail from both parents and their children meant loss of credibility to their detractors. They were stereotyped as squeaky-clean Americans, and making it known that they drank wine and liked Frank Zappa did not release them from the pigeonhole into which they had been slotted.

This image was only strengthened when they were invited to the White House for a photograph session with President Nixon in September 1972. Nixon held them up as a positive symbol for American youth, after which their image was firmly set in stone.

By this time, a new album, *A Song for You*, had been released, including the singles, "Hurting Each Other" (which reached number five on the American charts), "It's Going to Take Some Time" (number 14) and "Good-bye to

Love" (number seven in the U.S., number nine in Britain, and one of Karen's favorite tracks). The album was the last to give Jack Daugherty the production credit, as Richard was determined that his own work should bear his name. Daugherty's removal resulted in eight years of arguments in the courts but brought Richard the credit which was justly his.

In reality, it was impossible for them to be "normal" people, considering the workload they gave themselves and the pressures and obligations of the music business. The family unit that Richard and Karen made out of their entourage, which could number as many as 30 people, made it difficult for outsiders to become established—part of the reason that Karen dated only those people inside it. Although Richard gave her space for relationships, Karen tended to criticize Richard for his. Not only did she not like his time being taken up with relationships, but she seemed to think his girlfriends were not good enough for him. Agnes was also critical of Richard's girlfriends when he tried to introduce them into the family at Downey, and he soon became frustrated at not having a base of his own when he was not out on the road.

On the road was exactly where the Carpenters were for most of the five years starting in 1970. The unity of the band was sometimes fragile, as shows of individuality during a performance were strictly against orders and the band members felt pressured by such a rule. Mistakes could also bring a harsh reprimand from either Richard or Karen, as they insisted on the studio tracks being note perfect during performance. They were as hard on each other as they were on other band members, and there were regular arguments between them over some detail of a performance which one of them thought was below standard. They were lucky to lose only Karen's co-drummer during their five years of constant gigging; the Carpenters "family" was a very loyal one indeed.

Despite Richard's clear position as the one in charge of the musical side of the Carpenters, Karen was seen by those around her as in control of much of the management side.

They Died Too Young

Karen performs in the spotlight

Her direct confrontation of problems was as much a vice as a virtue, though, and her inflexibility was well-known. Her need to be in control extended, once more, to a dissatisfaction with her body. She made use of various slimming devices to keep her weight at the level that previous dieting had accomplished, but her health was good and no one worried as she began to miss meals and lose more weight.

Musically, 1973 started well for the Carpenters, with an oddball hit taken from the *Sesame Street* children's television show. "Sing" seemed to reinforce the image which the band was learning to live with and rose to number three at a time when several other singles, including the international smash "Tie a Yellow Ribbon 'Round the Old Oak Tree" by Tony Orlando and Dawn, were on the charts. A short way below "Sing" was "Twelfth of Never" by Donny Osmond, whose brother Alan, so Karen was stressing in interviews, was nothing more than a good friend.

The follow-up to "Sing" proved, once again, the effectiveness of the partnership between Richard and John Bettis. They wrote what many consider to be the definitive Carpenters song, "Yesterday Once More," which had the low notes that Richard knew created such intimacy between Karen and the listener, an anthem-like chorus, and nostalgic lyrics which Karen's rendition filled with relevance. It was the centerpiece (and the reprise) of an album split into contemporary songs and pop influences called aptly, *Now and Then*. The inclusion of classics like "Da Doo Ron Ron," "One Fine Day," and the Hank Williams song "Jambalaya (On the Border)," did not prevent the quality of "Yesterday Once More" from shining through, and it was a number-two hit on both sides of the Atlantic.

The touring schedule was broken in May 1973 by another visit to the White House, this time to play for the president. Even such seasoned performers were rather starstruck, and playing in such a small room was a restriction, but Richard Nixon and Willy Brandt, the West

They Died Too Young

German chancellor, who was on a state visit, enjoyed the selection of hits.

The next single was not from the new album; it was almost picked for them by popular demand during concerts and by pressure from A&M licenses around the world. It was "Top of the World" from *A Song for You*, which neither Richard nor Karen had thought had potential as a single. It brought them their second number one in America in November 1973—in Britain it held at number five, with the Osmonds' "Let Me In" taking the number one spot.

Relaxing in Los Angeles

SUPERSTAR

There was time for only one short break during 1973, and even that was a working holiday, playing two concerts while staying as the guests of IBM computers in a resort in Acapulco. Richard and Karen were with their partners of the time: Richard with the band's wardrobe manager, Maria Galeazzi, and Karen with David Alley, the Carpenters' personal assistant. The presence of Agnes and Harold on the "holiday" further indicated the constrictions placed upon Richard and Karen—neither relationship would last much beyond the holiday.

The commitment that Richard and Karen showed each other, the band, and their fans, gave them almost no time for the normal life to which they claimed to aspire. So great was their touring commitment during 1974 that there was no new Carpenters album that year. There was, however, a hits compilation, *The Singles, 1969–1973*, which was a guaranteed success. It put the band's astonishing success into clear perspective, and the quality and craftsmanship of its contents were indisputable. Karen's voice combined pinpoint accuracy and warmth with melodies and arrangements which were a cut above the trend-based music which occupied the majority of the charts. In Britain, where the band single-handedly kept A&M in the black, the album enjoyed a total of 17 weeks at number one, the longest stretch since Simon & Garfunkel's *Bridge Over Troubled Water*.

Critical response in Britain was similar to that in America, despite a sell-out tour in 1974. As far as the press was concerned, the current benchmark was the theatrical extravagance of glam rock, and the saccharine lyrics of the Carpenters were not something to declare an admiration for. Aware by now that they could not change critical opinion, Richard and Karen devised an ironic response at the end of the tour by sending gold rings to half a dozen record chiefs, inscribed on one side with the word "love" and on the other with a provocative insult.

They also managed to win an element of freedom that year by moving out of the family house. Although their new house was a mere five-minute drive away from their parents, it meant that Richard could carry on a relationship out of his mother's critical eye, but Karen proved no easier to live with. She always wanted to know his movements and hated it when he had someone stay. Nevertheless, the move gave them at least a little more personal space; Richard spent his small amount of spare time on his car collection, while Karen's collection of Disney characters and soft toys was continually increased by gifts from fans and friends.

It was about this time that Karen's friends and family started to notice her irregular eating habits and became aware that she had lost much of her full figure. The comments she got were complimentary at this stage; she was considered a healthy weight, and no one realized that her target weight was more extreme than the weight loss she had already achieved. She cut out almost all of the sweet foods that she had enjoyed from an early age and began to leave the greater part of her meals at the side of the plate.

Karen's boyfriend around this time was Mike Curb, owner of Curb records, whose sister Carol, a friend of Karen's, had been through the trauma of an eating disorder. Curb was one of the first people to be aware of Karen's increasing problem, and he would take her out for meals which he insisted that she finish. They were both too dedicated to their careers for

They Died Too Young

more than occasional dates, so Mike Curb could have only a temporary effect on Karen's growing habits.

As she turned 25, Karen had much to be thankful for and was the first to admit it, but she also suffered great feelings of inadequacy. She was never quite satisfied with the recordings which her admirers raved about, and although the number of men who were charmed by her attested to her personal and physical attractiveness, she was not happy with the way she looked. Jibes in the press about her dress sense and hairstyle increased these feelings of inadequacy. No amount of praise from friends or music business colleagues could dispel her feeling that she had won success under false pretenses.

As for her relationships, Karen obviously had a clear opinion of who was a match for her brother. Some would say that no one was good enough in her eyes. But her stated requirements for a partner of her own were also going to be difficult to fulfill. However, in the person of Terry Ellis her needs seemed to be satisfied. The British co-owner of Chrysalis Records and manager of the band Jethro Tull, he was intelligent, rich, and considered a wonder by the music industry. It was not long before Karen moved in with Ellis, and he began to take an interest in her career, causing concern at A&M that he would poach her for his record company, which, like A&M, catered mainly to progressive rock bands.

Ellis was surprised that A&M had not paid more attention to the Carpenters' live presentation. He made them take a look at themselves in comparison to other live acts and persuaded them to hire experts to work on their presentation. Richard and Ellis shared a mutual respect, and Ellis's objective view of the Carpenters' setup made Richard reconsider his relationship with their management of the time.

In the meantime, the music continued to flow from Richard's partnership with John Bettis. The next batch of singles came from the *Horizon* album of June 1975, the seventh

Richard and Karen in concert

record in six years. The jaunty "Please Mr. Postman" had been released earlier in the year, giving them another number-one hit in America, though it was held from a double top position by Pilot's "January" in Britain. "Solitaire" was, for many, a definitive version of the Neil Sedaka ballad, but the best overall Carpenters-style production was "Only Yesterday," with the combination of nostalgia and sweetness that their best-loved songs successfully blended. Again, the single fared better in America, reaching number four, with a more than creditable number seven-placing in Britain, considering the craze for songs like Mud's "Oh Boy," at the top of the charts. Richard and Karen were never completely happy with *Horizon*, feeling that it had been unnecessarily rushed. Despite this, the album easily went gold in America, and entered the British chart at number one.

Karen and Richard were not in the best of condition for the commitments they had to fulfill. Richard was becoming more and more reliant on the sleeping pills which he had started taking in safe amounts in late 1971. At first, they gave relief from the stresses of his work, but with the ever-increasing pressure, they became a bad habit that started to affect his waking hours, causing general tiredness and loss of concentration. Karen's growing obsession with reducing her weight had taken her past the compliments stage, and she began to look gaunt rather than slim. Their worsening tempers were an indication of a loss of equilibrium within the band as they began yet another tour, this time to promote the new album. They were brought closer to the edge than ever by what might have been considered a dangerous choice of a support act.

Neil Sedaka was not only a star in his own right, with a batch of quality songs to his name, but his stage performance was a lot more polished than the Carpenters', whose management gave him liberties which were usually taken only by the stars of the show. Richard was so desperate that in August 1975 he fired Sedaka. The press had a field day, for Sedaka could claim, quite legitimately from some points of view, that he had been kicked out because he was too good.

The experience gave a jolt to the whole Carpenters' "family" and resulted in the dismissal of their manager. Terry Ellis agreed to take over on a strictly temporary basis and immediately tried to implement some new performance techniques for the band. But he was too late to save the tour. Karen was down to about 80 pounds and was too exhausted to continue with the Japanese and European leg of the tour. Her illness was officially declared to be an inflammation of the colon, though the possibility of anorexia nervosa was brought up by some who had heard of the condition, although most people knew little about it at the time.

Karen was kept in a hospital for a short time before being allowed home on the conditions that she rest and eat properly. She had recovered somewhat by October, though she was still too weak, and she and Ellis took a vacation before resuming life back in Los Angeles. Unfortunately their time together made them realize that, despite their strong feelings for each other, there were differences between them that could not be surmounted. The principal differences concerned their opposite lifestyles: Ellis was a social being, a restaurant lover and wine buff, while Karen veered toward nights in with the television and a TV dinner. Karen returned, distraught, to the house she shared with Richard, feeling that she would never find anyone as right for her as Ellis.

Her residual weakness made her susceptible to minor ailments, though the natural strength of her voice rarely failed her. The habit of five years' constant activity was one which she found impossible to break, and she was soon back to her old punishing work schedule. Richard, too, found the notion of rest very difficult, and his intake of pills had increased dramatically. If someone had been able to persuade them to take a serious break from work, in the understanding that their career was not in the usual pop mold and that they had

They Died Too Young

many years of potential in them, they might have been able to escape the trouble that lay ahead.

The Carpenters were back on the road in the spring of 1976, picking up where they had left off. On the European leg of the tour Karen fell for John Adrian, an executive of the promotion company sent to take special care of favored (and lucrative) clients. The affair was stopped in its tracks by a phone call from America to A&M (U.K.), which brought about Adrian's departure on a "free holiday" to the West Indies. Of course the relationship might well have come to nothing—Karen did have strict requirements for a partner—but fortunately, she never knew about the devious means taken to end the affair.

Karen felt the need to make a break from the confinement of her family and the Downey area. She had been considering such a move for a while, but the thought of leaving what had always been the safest of harbors for her was difficult. The split with Terry Ellis was the spur she needed to gain true independence, to move in the same circles as her other show business friends, and to escape the pressure from her mother. She bought and combined two apartments on Avenue of the Stars, Century City, and moved in at the end of 1976.

The large space was filled with her stuffed toys, and the 26-year-old was as proud as anyone who sets up a home on their own. There were still regular visits to and from the rest of the family, and the ties, though loosened, were still strong. Her independence allowed Karen to lapse back into her non-eating habits, and an employee recalled later that the kitchen cupboards were always empty. However, she enjoyed her wealth and independence by going on shopping trips and meeting her friends in the Beverly Hills area. Although many of her pals, like Olivia Newton-John, were from the world of show business, Karen maintained friendships with others outside the business. She was an avid writer of cards and letters when she was touring and always remembered birthdays and other anniversaries.

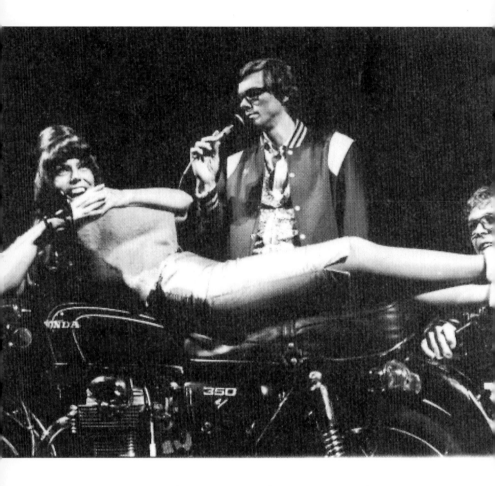

*The Carpenters' stage routine for
the song "Greased Lightning"*

HURTING EACH OTHER

"A Kind of Hush (All over the World)" was the only hit single from the album *Kind of Hush* that the Carpenters released in 1976. They had been considering a change of direction in the packaging of their music, and earlier in the year, hoping to attract a television audience, had signed Jerry Weintraub, who had all the right television contacts, to be their new manager.

Weintraub had a theory about major artists' longevity, which had been borne out by his experiences with Frank Sinatra, Neil Diamond, and Bob Dylan. He considered that the Carpenters were in a mid-career lull and that they needed a fresh impetus to regain the attention of fans whose tastes were changing as they grew older. Their new manager's clout won Richard and Karen their first television special in December 1976, despite resistance from company executives who took the Carpenters' press image, rather than their enormous fan-base, as a standpoint. The TV show was a great success, and they were assured of the chance of similar ventures. Richard and Karen responded positively to Weintraub's fresh ideas, despite their growing health problems.

Weintraub organized the hiring of Joe Layton, a Broadway producer who had worked with other pop artists, and he designed a show for the Carpenters which brought them out from behind their instruments. Out went the static performances of the last six years, and in came theatrical routines involving costume changes and props, such as a motorcycle,

35

that Richard rode onstage for the introduction of "Greased Lightning." The critics didn't know whether it was a brave or foolish move, but the halls were packed and the audiences appreciative.

Karen developed a father/daughter rapport, as well as a manager/artist relationship, with Weintraub. He soon became aware of her state of health, but her strength of purpose and good humor misled him, along with many others, as to the seriousness of her condition. Her family and the band, however, became aware that Karen was in the grip of a potentially major problem. Richard tried persuasion, arguing, shouting. Members of the band took her out for meals and begged her to eat. Her father told her she was just a bag of bones. But Karen had entered a phase of single-minded determination to reach a dangerously low target weight. One of the possible causes of anorexia is the sufferer's need for attention, and perhaps by starving herself, Karen was getting attention that, to her mind, she might not otherwise receive.

The Carpenters 1977 album release was a further source of worry for them, as they wanted to regain the form they felt they had lost over the past two records. *Passage* did not realize their hopes, however, and was the first album not to go "gold" — or sell half a million copies. Its most successful single release, "Calling Occupants of Interplanetary Craft," hung around outside the American top 30, though it made number eight in Britain later that year. It was not that there was a lack of good material — "All You Get from Love is a Love Song" and "Sweet Sweet Smile" were signature Carpenters songs, but the singles-buying public was high on disco fever, and on the album charts, Fleetwood Mac was at the top for over half of the year with *Rumours*.

For Richard and Karen, who had spent so many years concentrating on their music, the loss of sales was extremely worrisome. They had always been aware of the fickle nature of pop music, but the additional pressure hit their weakened dispositions hard. Richard's intake of sleeping pills was causing his hands to shake, and he would wake up during the night to take even more. He acknowledged his problem in 1977 and went into the hospital for a detoxification program, but although his system was cleansed, the problem remained, and he began a two-year battle to free himself of the addiction.

One project that Richard had had in mind for several years was an album of Christmas songs, an idea which suited the Carpenters' image, as well as being an ideal platform for Karen's voice. Richard knew he was in no state to handle the arrangements and production all on his own, so he got specialist help in both departments. *Christmas Portrait* would become a regular Christmas seller and brought Karen back in contact with Tom Bahler, who with his brother John organized the choral work for the album. It was the Bahlers who had organized Richard and Karen's Ford Motors deal back in 1969, and their careers had taken parallel paths ever since.

Karen and Tom began a relationship and found much in common. There was of course the issue of Karen's eating, which Tom tried to deal with. Karen refused to see there was a problem, but it didn't seem to spoil their romance. What eventually broke them up was the fact that Tom had a child from a previous relationship with a married woman. Morally, Karen could not come to terms with this part of his past, and the affair cooled, although they were to remain friends.

The other vinyl release of 1978 was a second greatest hits collection compiled for the British market, *The Carpenters Singles 1974-1978*. It was a good selection, featuring many songs previously released as singles only in America.

Richard reached his lowest ebb during a tour in September that year, when he realized he couldn't continue with the live shows. His playing had suffered so much from the effects of the sleeping pills, that he had already cut out many of the more intricate arrangements, and he was terrified of cracking up completely on stage. He and

Karen Carpenter

Karen paid off the band, not guessing at the time that, at ages 31 and 28 respectively, they had played the last concert of their careers.

Karen flew to London to honor a promotional commitment at the end of 1978, with the excuse that Richard had the flu. She shouldered her responsibility professionally, appearing on a television show to sing a selection of hits. Richard knew that he was useless to the partnership as well as to himself and booked himself in for a six-week stay at a Kansas treatment center in January 1979.

When Karen visited him after a couple of weeks, he was in the middle of the initial, most difficult period of withdrawal, and there were angry exchanges between the two as he tried to get Karen to admit to her problem, bringing up the dreaded name, anorexia nervosa. Richard's pleas came on top of cajoling from Jerry Weintraub, so Karen arranged to have some medical tests. But Richard was right in believing that until she had a realistic mental image of herself, no one would be able to help her. Weintraub had good reason to be concerned. He was the manager of two gifted artists, among the top earning musicians of their time, and they were both disintegrating in front of his eyes.

More on Karen's mind at that moment was the offer of a solo venture with producer Phil Ramone, the man behind previous hits for Paul Simon and Billy Joel. Richard didn't like the idea at all, but he didn't have the right to stop Karen from taking on an independent project, and he was in no condition to offer an alternative with himself. In fact he would take the whole of the year to recover properly, staying with friends around the country before returning to Downey to complete a full physical and mental convalescence. His structured recovery helped him to understand the pressure he and Karen had been under for years, and he was able to take a longer view of his career, not worrying too much about the lack of an annual album. His sister was not so lucky.

Karen performs solo

GOOD-BYE TO LOVE

Karen flew to New York for initial meetings with Phil Ramone, though she had to leave early for a minor ear operation, due to complications from a burst eardrum during a flight a couple of years earlier. A&M was positive about her making a record without Richard at the helm, but she felt both insecure and excited and needed Richard's blessing to go ahead. He gave it reluctantly, though he had one warning: "Don't do anything disco." She returned to New York in May 1979 and took up residence in a hotel for the duration of the recording.

Phil Ramone's trademark style was more rock-based than anything the Carpenters had attempted, and he felt sure that he could bring out a maturity in Karen that he thought she lacked in her usual work. He wanted her to sing from experience, rather than from the fantasy world he saw the Carpenters as representing, and his choice of material had a rougher, more sensual edge: songs like "My Body Keeps Changing My Mind" and "If I Had You." The pressure Ramone put on her in the studio was in complete contrast to her working regime with Richard, who got the best results from simply letting her sing. Her difficulties were compounded by several minor ailments stemming from her general weakness.

At one point Ramone found her passed out on her hotel-room floor. She admitted that she had been taking Quaaludes, the same pills that had gotten Richard in so much trouble. What she did not admit was that she was

41

also taking thyroid medication, which sped up her metabolism. For an anorexic to put an extra strain on her heart, on top of the strain caused by lack of nourishment, was extremely dangerous. If a doctor had known what she was doing, a period of observed hospitalization would have been the only sensible course of action. Instead she was living in a city where she had few friends, working on a record which she felt had to be successful to restore the Carpenters' record sales. Half a million dollars had been invested in the project by herself and A&M, and she desperately wanted it to pay off.

The result was extremely disappointing. Despite the end-of-recording jubilation and Karen's positive reaction to the finished masters in early 1980, Herb Alpert knew that the album was not good enough to release. The songs were nowhere near the quality of the Carpenters' usual output. Karen's voice was as perfect as always, but it didn't mesh with the brash dance arrangements of Phil Ramone. Richard thought the problem was due to a basic mismatch between the contemporary ideas of Ramone and Karen's classic style. Although mixing two different styles can be successful if there is some indefinable "magic" to bring them together, the consensus was that the magic was lacking for Karen and Phil Ramone. As a result, the album was denied the chance of a public airing, although Richard would include several remixed tracks from the project on a release after Karen's death.

After a short break with Olivia Newton-John, Karen declared herself ready to go back to the studio with her revitalized brother. He refused to begin anything until she recovered some weight, for she had lost yet more during her stay in New York. The threat worked, and Karen saw a specialist and tipped the scales at over 100 pounds. But there was still no acceptance of the underlying reasons for her need to lose weight. She was happy and positive in the spring of 1980, and her friends were relieved to see some flesh on her bones. She even submitted to a blind date organized by one of her friends, and so met Tom Burris.

They Died Too Young

Burris was charming, a lawyer, and thus independent. He and Karen fell head over heels for each other and were engaged after two months. Richard had more trouble getting to like Burris; he had gotten along well with several of Karen's partners, maybe because they had almost all been in the music business.

The sumptuous summer wedding took place at the Beverly Hills Hotel and the space was designed to resemble an English country garden. Richard led a 40-piece orchestra, and the assembled show business guests and friends were treated to "Because We Are in Love," a song written and recorded especially for the occasion. The honeymoon couple flew to the beautiful island of Bora Bora, and everyone involved in Karen's life prayed for a happy ending for the newlyweds.

While they were away, Richard prepared material for what he hoped would be the 1981 comeback album, *Made in America*. It promised a new, positive stand along with the usual wistfulness, and it included "Strength of a Woman" and "Because We Are in Love (The Wedding Song)." The single "Touch Me When We're Dancing" reached number 16 in America in August. Considering the four years between *Passage* and *Made In America,* which had seen the rise of a new breed of American rock, as well as the punk and new wave movements in Britain, the response to the album was encouraging.

The news about Karen's marriage, however, was not as heartening. Tom Burris's more adventurous view of life involved the great outdoors to an extent which the home-loving Karen could not handle, despite, or maybe because of, her life as a traveling musician. Her long hours in the studio, followed by a promotional tour of the new album, gave them little time to get to know each other in depth, and Burris walked out of the Carpenter house in November 1981, never to see Karen alive again.

A great part of the problem in their marriage must have been Karen's growing awareness that she had to do something about her health. In October 1981, just before Tom Burris walked out of her life, she worked up the courage to contact Dr. Steven Levenkron, an authority on eating disorders to whom Karen had spoken a couple of years before. By now she was desperate enough to seek help. Levenkron's experience with anorexics had directed him to a method of straight-talking, strictly observed treatment, and he told Karen that he could only help her if she moved to New York for six months of regular sessions with him. In November, Karen flew to meet the man who she hoped could cure the monster which had taken over her life and was now endangering it.

Levenkron had to deal with a 31-year-old woman who was taking a combination of thyroid tablets and laxatives, as well as having difficulty taking in food. Karen had allowed her condition to deteriorate to such a level that several of his colleagues doubted she had any chance of survival. At the beginning of their sessions she weighed 78 pounds.

Every morning Levenkron would work at breaking down her dependency on drugs and talk about her feelings of conflict with Richard and her family. But Richard, aware of how well residential treatment had worked for him, believed she should be under constant supervision. While living in New York, Karen managed a social life with the friends she had made there and others who came to visit her. But she was not able to return to a normal eating pattern, and after three months there was very little success to report. She had stopped using laxatives for a while and her weight went up, but she soon relapsed and looked as thin as when she first arrived in New York. She returned to California for a recording break in April, laying down what would be her final song, "Now."

Back in New York, Karen was forced to enter a hospital, where the staff were obliged to feed her directly into the bloodstream, since her digestive tract was too damaged by her eating habits to allow normal digestion. The amazing thing was that her disposition remained good throughout most of her illness. She was bright and cheerful with her friends, and Steven Levenkron could not help liking this tragic but charming woman.

She left the hospital after two months in November 1982; she weighed 90 pounds, had been in treatment for a year, and decided she wanted to go home. Back in Los Angeles it was clear that Karen was not on the road to recovery, despite her protestations to the contrary. Although she was supposed to rest, she had returned to her normal active life.

When Richard drove her back home after a meal on February 1, 1983, Karen was in high spirits, looking forward to a new period of work. Two days later she visited her mother and they discussed washing machines and a shopping expedition to buy clothes for her new weight of 108 pounds. She stayed overnight as she regularly did, and the following morning Agnes prepared breakfast. She went to call Karen at 10 minutes to nine and found her collapsed in the bedroom. It was February 4, 1983. Karen's heart had given up after years of punishment, and the autopsy report gave the cause of death as heart failure due to anorexia nervosa.

Karen Carpenter was buried four days later, and hundreds of people crammed into the small church. Her coffin contained Tom Burris's wedding ring, which he had placed there. The inscription on the marble crypt read, "Karen 1950–1983. A star on earth. A star in heaven."

Karen Carpenter remains a positive influence for other sufferers of the disease, helping them with the foundations set up after her death. Her name is enshrined with a star on the Hollywood Walk of Fame. In her recordings and in previously unreleased tracks mastered by Richard since her death, she bequeaths a golden voice which has been discovered by a new generation of fans.

CHRONOLOGY

1950 Karen Carpenter born to parents Agnes and Harold on March 2.

1965 Karen, her older brother Richard, and Wes Jacobs form the Richard Carpenter Trio and play together at dances and weddings.

1966 Karen is signed to a small record label, Magic Lamp, where she releases one unsuccessful single.

1967 After winning a "Battle of the Bands" contest, the Carpenters sign a contract with RCA from which they are later released without producing an album.

1969 Richard and Karen sign a contract with A&M records; their first album, *Offering* (renamed *Ticket to Ride*), is released.

1970 "Close to You" reaches number one six weeks after its release and spends four weeks at the top; Carpenters win Grammys for Best New Artist and Best Contemporary Vocal Group.

1973 *The Singles: 1969–73* is the number one album for 17 weeks; the Carpenters tour continuously, playing to sold out crowds; Karen's weight loss first attracts attention.

1979 Karen's attempt to launch a solo career is unsuccessful.

1980 Sees a weight specialist and brings her weight up to 100 pounds; marries lawyer Tom Burris at the Beverly Hills Hotel.

1981 *Made in America*, the Carpenters' last album of new material, is released; husband Tom Burris leaves Karen.

1982 Hospitalized and fed intraveneously when treatment for anorexia nervosa with Dr. Steven Levenkron proves unsuccessful.

1983 Karen collapses in her parents' home in California on February 4 and dies of heart failure due to anorexia nervosa.

"Karen 1950–1983. A star on earth. A star in heaven."

INDEX